W9-CAD-109

Exploring Countries

Indonesia

BLAINE WISEMAN

AV2 BY WEIGL
MEDIA ENHANCED BOOKS
ADDED VALUE • AUDIO VISUAL

www.av2books.com

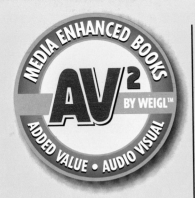

AV² provides enriched content that supplements and complements this book. Weigl's AV² books strive to create inspired learning and engage young minds in a total learning experience.

Your AV² Media Enhanced books come alive with...

Audio
Listen to sections of the book read aloud.

Key Words
Study vocabulary, and complete a matching word activity.

Video
Watch informative video clips.

Quizzes
Test your knowledge.

Go to www.av2books.com, and enter this book's unique code.

BOOK CODE

E 8 2 4 4 9 9

Embedded Weblinks
Gain additional information for research.

Slide Show
View images and captions, and prepare a presentation.

AV² by Weigl brings you media enhanced books that support active learning.

Try This!
Complete activities and hands-on experiments.

... and much, much more!

Published by AV² by Weigl
350 5th Avenue, 59th Floor
New York, NY 10118
Website: www.av2books.com

Library of Congress Cataloging-in-Publication Data

Names: Wiseman, Blaine, author.
Title: Indonesia / Blaine Wiseman.
Description: New York, NY : AV2 by Weigl, 2016. | Series: Exploring countries | Includes index. | Description based on print version record and CIP data provided by publisher; resource not viewed.
Identifiers: LCCN 2015049873 (print) | LCCN 2015049793 (ebook) | ISBN 9781489646125 (Multi-User eBook) | ISBN 9781489646118 (hard cover : alk. paper) | ISBN 9781489650276 (soft cover : alk. paper)
Subjects: LCSH: Indonesia--Juvenile literature. | Indonesia--Description and travel--Juvenile literature.
Classification: LCC DS615 (print) | LCC DS615 .W57 2016 (ebook) | DDC 959.8--dc23
LC record available at http://lccn.loc.gov/2015049873

Printed in the United States of America in Brainerd, Minnesota
1 2 3 4 5 6 7 8 9 20 19 18 17 16

032016
150316

Project Coordinator Heather Kissock
Art Director Terry Paulhus

Photo Credits
Every reasonable effort has been made to trace ownership and to obtain permission to reprint copyright material. The publishers would be pleased to have any errors or omissions brought to their attention so that they may be corrected in subsequent printings.

Weigl acknowledges Corbis Images and Getty Images as its primary photo suppliers for this title.

Contents

Indonesia Overview

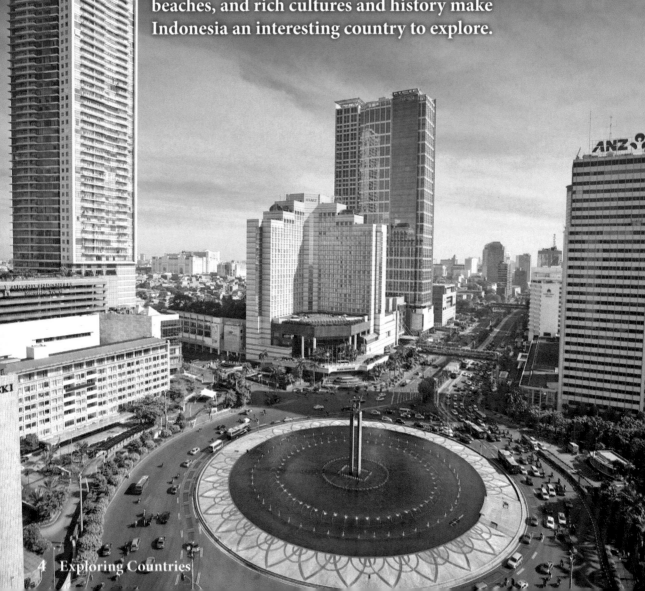

Indonesia is a country made up of about 17,500 islands in Southeast Asia. The islands cover a large area along the equator. For thousands of years, people have been sailing to Indonesia to trade and settle. The country is between two oceans, the Indian Ocean to the west and the Pacific to the east. The mainland of Asia is to the north, and the continent of Australia is to the south. Today, Indonesia's population is the fourth-largest of any nation in the world. Powerful volcanoes helped shape Indonesia's land. Thick jungles, beautiful beaches, and rich cultures and history make Indonesia an interesting country to explore.

The only Sumatran tigers in nature live on the Indonesian island of Sumatra. They number fewer than 400.

The waters around Indonesia's Molucca, or Maluku, Islands are home to colorful sea life, including clownfish.

Bali is often called the "Island of a Thousand Temples." Pura Taman Saraswati Temple is in Ubud.

Parades in the city of Jakarta feature many of the country's cultures.

The juicy mangosteen fruit is native to Indonesia.

Exploring Indonesia

Indonesia covers 735,358 square miles (1,904,569 square kilometers). It is the world's largest island country and the biggest nation in Southeast Asia. Indonesia shares land borders with the countries of Malaysia, Papua New Guinea, and East Timor. Kalimantan, the Indonesian portion of the island of Borneo, touches Malaysia. The island of New Guinea is made up of Indonesia in the west and Papua New Guinea in the east. East Timor is a small country bordering Indonesia on the island of Timor. The rest of Indonesia borders the seas and oceans surrounding its coastlines.

Myanmar

Thailand

Laos

Cambodia

Vietnam

South China Sea

Malaysia

Sumatra

Jakarta

Java

Indian Ocean

Sumatra

Jakarta

Map Legend

Indonesia

Land

Water

Kapuas River

Puncak Jaya

Sumatra

Capital City

SCALE

| 500 Miles |
| 500 Kilometers |

Sumatra

Sumatra is the largest Indonesian island. New Guinea and Borneo are bigger, but not all of their land is Indonesian. Sumatra covers 182,543 square miles (472,784 sq. km).

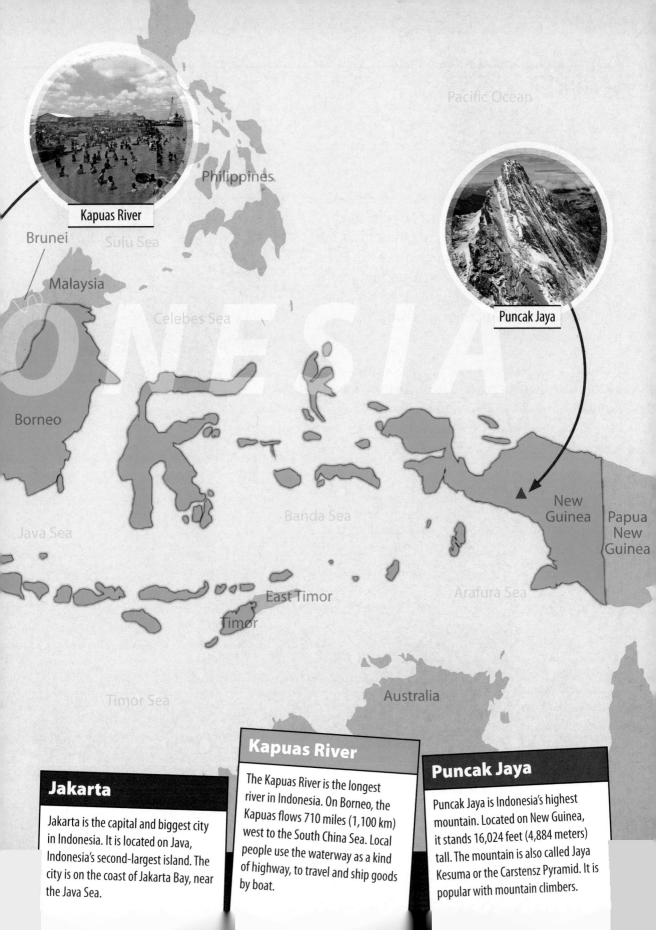

Pacific Ocean

Philippines

Kapuas River

Brunei

Sulu Sea

Malaysia

Celebes Sea

Borneo

Puncak Jaya

New
Guinea

Papua
New
Guinea

Banda Sea

Java Sea

Arafura Sea

East Timor

Timor

Timor Sea

Australia

Jakarta

Jakarta is the capital and biggest city in Indonesia. It is located on Java, Indonesia's second-largest island. The city is on the coast of Jakarta Bay, near the Java Sea.

Kapuas River

The Kapuas River is the longest river in Indonesia. On Borneo, the Kapuas flows 710 miles (1,100 km) west to the South China Sea. Local people use the waterway as a kind of highway, to travel and ship goods by boat.

Puncak Jaya

Puncak Jaya is Indonesia's highest mountain. Located on New Guinea, it stands 16,024 feet (4,884 meters) tall. The mountain is also called Jaya Kesuma or the Carstensz Pyramid. It is popular with mountain climbers.

LAND AND CLIMATE

Many of Indonesia's islands were formed over millions of years by the eruptions of volcanoes. Indonesia has more volcanoes than any other country in the world. Often, when a volcano erupts, hot melted rock called lava comes out of the volcano's top. The lava then hardens as it cools, which creates new land.

Indonesia has so many volcanoes because of its location. Earth's surface is divided into a number of pieces called tectonic plates. The edges of several plates are below Indonesia. As the plates slowly move, melted rock from deep inside Earth can come to the surface. This causes volcanic eruptions. The movement of plates below Indonesia also causes many earthquakes. In recent times, earthquakes in the country have caused a great deal of damage.

Indonesia has more than 130 active volcanoes, including Krakatau, which is on a small island between Java and Sumatra.

Lakes and rivers are plentiful in Indonesia. The country's largest lake is Lake Toba, located on Sumatra. This lake covers about 440 square miles (1,140 sq. km). Major rivers include the Batanghari on Sumatra, the Solo on Java, and the Mamberamo on the Indonesian part of New Guinea.

Indonesia is one of the world's most heavily forested regions. Trees cover more than half of the land. Indonesia has more tropical rainforest than any other country except Brazil in South America and Congo in Africa. Large tropical rainforests in Indonesia are located on the islands of New Guinea, Borneo, and Sumatra. A tropical rainforest is a forest of tall trees in a region where the weather is warm and damp year-round.

Indonesia's climate is generally very hot and wet. In areas at low **elevation** near the coast, temperatures can rise to 100° Fahrenheit (38° Celsius) or more. At higher elevations, such as in mountainous areas, temperatures are often lower. There is sometimes snow in the high mountains of New Guinea. Wet weather is common in most parts of the country. The rainiest season is between December and March. Powerful **monsoons** gather water from the oceans and drop it on Indonesia's islands.

> The peaks of Batukau, Sangiyang, and Pohen overlook the green rice terraces of the Balinese village of Jatiluwih. Thousands of years ago, farmers cut the terraces, or flat areas, into the hillsides to improve the land for growing crops.

Land and Climate BY THE NUMBERS

3,200 Miles
Distance Indonesia spans from east to west. (5,100 km)

More Than 120 Inches
Total annual rainfall in the wettest regions of Indonesia. (305 centimeters)

34,000 Miles
Length of Indonesia's coastline, which is longer than any country's except Canada's. (55,000 km)

MORE THAN 130,000
Death toll in Indonesia from a **tsunami** caused by an earthquake in the Indian Ocean in 2004.

PLANTS AND ANIMALS

Indonesia has many **species** of plants and animals that live nowhere else in the world. Some species can be found only on certain islands. Borneo, Sumatra, and New Guinea provide some of Earth's most diverse **ecosystems**.

Indonesian rainforests are home to the world's largest flowers, which grow on the rafflesia plant. Durian trees in these rainforests produce a sweet but foul-smelling fruit. Rare animal species, such as orangutans and proboscis monkeys, swing from the trees in Borneo and Sumatra. Komodo dragons exist on five small islands in southeastern Indonesia. The Javan rhinoceros is found only in a small area of Java.

Mangroves, which originated in Southeast Asia, are common in Indonesia. These trees and shrubs grow in salty slow-moving waters in tropical areas near the coast. The largest mangrove forests in the world are found in Indonesia.

5,000 Number of orchid species in Indonesia.

24 Pounds Weight of the heaviest known rafflesia flowers. (11 kilograms)

60 Number of Javan rhinoceroses left in nature.

4 Number of continents besides Asia to which mangroves spread because their seeds floated on ocean currents.

The Komodo dragon can weigh up to 300 pounds (135 kg). It is the world's largest lizard.

NATURAL RESOURCES

Petroleum, or oil, and natural gas are Indonesia's most valuable natural resources. Most of these resources are found off the coast in the Java Sea and South China Sea. Indonesia has large coal deposits, and it **exports** more coal than any other country except Australia. It also has large **reserves** of tin, nickel, and copper.

Rich soil is another important natural resource. About 13 percent of the country's land is suitable for growing crops. Much of this land is used for **subsistence farming**.

The lumber in Indonesia's forests is a natural resource. However, in recent years Indonesia has lost large areas of its rainforests. Many trees have been cut down so that the wood can be sold. Others have been burned to clear land for farming.

The most common crop grown in Indonesia is rice.

Natural Resources BY THE NUMBERS

1.5 Million
Number of acres of rainforest Indonesia is losing every year to **deforestation**. (610,000 hectares)

1%
Portion of the world's oil produced in Indonesia.

31 Billion Tons
Size of Indonesia's coal reserves. (28 billion metric tons)

TOURISM

In 2014, almost 10 million foreign tourists came to Indonesia to enjoy its rich culture, history, and natural beauty. The tourism industry is important to Indonesia's **economy**. Tourism creates jobs for many Indonesians. Visitors spend money on tours, hotels, transportation, meals, and entertainment.

Indonesia's clear waters and sandy beaches are two of its major attractions. Resorts and beaches on the island of Bali are popular with many visitors. In fact, Bali is one of the world's most common honeymoon destinations. Tourists enjoy surfing and hiking there. The nearby Gili Islands, with a **hatchery** for green sea and loggerhead turtles, are known as the "Turtle Capital of the World."

On the Gili Islands, the only way to get around is by bicycle or horse-drawn cart.

Guided tours on Bali rivers offer kayaking, tubing, and rafting.

Indonesia's 51 national parks attract large numbers of tourists. More than 60,000 people visit Komodo National Park each year. The park, which spans three small islands, is the home of many Komodo dragons. At Bromo Tengerr Semeru National Park on Java, plumes of smoke and ash rise from volcanoes.

Religious temples of different sizes and ages are found throughout the country. These historic sites attract visitors to Bali, Java, and many other areas. Borobudur Temple, built in the eighth and ninth centuries on Java, receives about 2.5 million visitors each year.

Tourists also visit Prambanan Temple on Java. Built in the ninth century, the temple features buildings that honor Vishnu, Brahma, and Shiva, the three gods in **Hinduism**. Prambanan's central tower rises to a height of 150 feet (47 m). The temple is the largest Hindu monument in the country.

Tanjung Puting National Park in Borneo is home to more than 30,000 orangutans. This is the world's largest orangutan population in nature.

5,700
Number of Komodo dragons in Komodo National Park.

8 Number of **UNESCO** World Heritage sites in Indonesia, including Prambanan Temple.

Almost $10 Billion
Amount spent by tourists in Indonesia in 2014.

INDUSTRY

More than one-third of Indonesia's workers are farmers. Many others are employed in industry. Major industries include manufacturing, processing agricultural products, producing oil and gas, and mining.

Palm oil, cocoa, rubber, forest products, and coffee are Indonesia's largest agricultural exports. The country is the world's largest producer of palm oil. This oil is used in baked goods, ice cream, and detergents. Indonesia is the world's second-largest exporter of tin and third-largest copper exporter.

For many years, Indonesia sold much of its oil and gas to other countries. Today, as the population grows, more oil and gas is used in Indonesia. Experts predict the country's oil reserves will last only another 23 years. That means **renewable sources** of energy may be important for the country's future. The Indonesian government has set a goal of increasing renewable energy from 5 percent to 25 percent of total energy used by the year 2025.

39%
Portion of Indonesia's workers employed in agriculture.

13% Percent of workers in Indonesia with jobs in industry.

23RD Indonesia's rank in world production of petroleum.

Indonesia provides half the world's palm oil. Palm oil is made from a tree fruit called oil palm.

GOODS AND SERVICES

Nearly half of Indonesia's workers are employed in service jobs. These people provide services to others. Service workers include tour guides, teachers, doctors and nurses, bankers, hotel staffs, airport workers, and people who drive buses or taxis.

Indonesia's food service industry is one of the fastest-growing parts of the economy. As cities in Indonesia grow, their residents rely more on restaurants and food delivery services. This creates jobs for cooks, servers, and other workers. Some restaurants in Indonesia are part of international chains. However, more than 90 percent of restaurants are independent businesses.

Indonesia **imports** more petroleum products than any other type of goods. Other major imports include electronics, such as computers and telephones. The country also buys automobile parts, used to manufacture cars.

Tourism businesses, such as hotel restaurants, employ more than 3 million people in Indonesia.

INDIGENOUS PEOPLES

Scientists who study **fossils** found in Indonesia believe that humans have lived in the area for about 1.7 million years. The remains of bones found on Java led to the discovery of an ancient species of humans, called *Homo erectus*. The remains themselves became known as Java Man. Carvings on shells found on Java show that *Homo erectus* might have been living on the islands now known as Indonesia as recently as 430,000 years ago.

Modern humans, or *Homo sapiens*, began living in Southeast Asia about 50,000 years ago. Over time, different groups of people settled different areas of what is today Indonesia. These groups of indigenous peoples may have traded with each other, but they remained mostly independent. This led to the various languages and cultures still found in Indonesia today.

Indigenous Peoples BY THE NUMBERS

1891
Year that Java Man's bones were discovered at Trinil, Java.

ABOUT 50 MILLION
Estimated total of indigenous peoples in Indonesia today.

Fewer Than 1,000
Number of Dayak Benuaq tribe members in eastern Borneo.

The indigenous Tengger people live in Bromo Tengger Semeru National Park on Java.

EARLY SETTLERS

Many of Indonesia's early settlers were able to survive on local natural resources. These people grew rice on Java. They fished on Borneo and Sumatra.

Beginning nearly 2,000 years ago, traders from other parts of Southeast Asia and from India or China visited Indonesia's islands by boat. Over time, the cultures of these traders influenced the local communities. The largest early influence on Indonesian cultures was from India. Indian traders and others brought religions such as **Buddhism** and Hinduism to Indonesia. These religions shared many aspects with traditional Indonesian beliefs at the time.

In the sixth, seventh, and eighth centuries, many small and medium-sized kingdoms formed in Indonesia. The biggest was the Sumatran kingdom of Srivijaya. Another powerful kingdom was the Shailendra **dynasty** in central Java. Rulers in this dynasty built the Buddhist Borobudur Temple.

Early Settlers BY THE NUMBERS

MORE THAN 500
Number of Buddha statues in Borobudur Temple.

671 Year that Chinese Buddhist I-ching first visited Indonesia and wrote about the Srivijaya kingdom.

About 750–850
Years when the Shailendra dynasty was at the height of its power.

About 2 million cubic feet (57,000 cubic meters) of stone was used to build Borobudur.

THE AGE OF EXPLORATION

ontact with other cultures increased in the 13th century. The Javanese kingdom of the ruler named Kertanagara was growing, and more traders were coming to the island. In 1292, soldiers of the Mongol general Kublai Khan invaded Java and were defeated. The kingdom moved to the city of Majapahit and grew under Kertanagara's **descendants**.

Majapahit warriors in the 14th century used a type of knife called a kris dagger. The blade was usually wavy, which made it more dangerous.

As early as the 11th century, Muslim traders from India were sailing to Indonesia. Muslims are people who follow the religion of Islam. By the end of the 13th century, Islamic kingdoms were developing in Indonesia. The most powerful was the Samudra-Pasai kingdom in northern Sumatra. Its power was based on trade. Samudra-Pasai later became the kingdom of Aceh.

Singhasari Temple in East Java was built in memory of the Javanese ruler Kertanagara.

In the 15th and 16th centuries, European countries sent explorers sailing all over the world in order to claim new lands and create **empires**. In 1511, Portugal conquered the kingdom of Malacca, which was on the Southeast Asian mainland in present-day Malaysia. This brought the Portuguese closer to Sumatra. The Muslim kingdom of Aceh asked for help from the Ottoman Empire, a Muslim dynasty based in Turkey. However, the Ottomans could not keep out European traders and conquerors.

Cloves and other valuable spices brought many foreigners to the Molucca Islands. For this reason, the Moluccas came to be known as the Spice Islands. European powers wanted control of the islands and their valuable spices. The Spanish, English, and Dutch fought over the area. In the early 1600s, the Dutch East India Company of the Netherlands sent ships to the Spice Islands. Dutch control over Indonesia's trade, land, and people grew. Except for brief periods of time, the Netherlands ruled Indonesia until the mid-20th century.

European explorers sailed to the Molucca Islands for spices such as nutmeg and mace.

POPULATION

In 2015, more than 255 million people lived in Indonesia. The country has more people than any other nation in the world except for China, India, and the United States. Since 2010, Indonesia has grown by more than 15 million people.

A large portion of Indonesians are children or teenagers. More than 25 percent of people are younger than 15 years old. This compares to less than 20 percent in the United States. The average age of people in Indonesia is about 30 years old, eight years younger than the average for Americans.

Most of Indonesia's population can be found on only a few islands. Java, with 141 million residents, is home to more than half of Indonesia's people. The population of Sumatra numbers more than 50 million. These two islands contain the country's five biggest cities. Jakarta has more than 10 million residents. Surabaya, Bandung, and Medan each have more than 2 million people. More than 1.6 million people live in Semarang.

About 6,000
Number of unpopulated islands in Indonesia.

94% Portion of people in Indonesia age 15 and older who can read and write.

53% Portion of the population that lives in **urban** areas.

The populations of Jakarta and other cities are growing quickly.

POLITICS AND GOVERNMENT

During World War II, Japan seized Indonesia from the Dutch. When Japan was defeated and World War II ended in 1945, Indonesia declared its independence. However, the Netherlands tried to regain control, and the Dutch did not agree to independence for Indonesia until 1949.

Indonesia's first president after independence was Sukarno. In 1957, he announced his own form of government called Guided Democracy. Sukarno used the military and the power of the presidency to control Indonesia. An attempted **coup d'état** in 1965 led to the fall of Sukarno, and an army general named Suharto became president. Suharto ruled Indonesia until 1998. In that year, large protests by people unhappy with his government forced Suharto to resign.

Under Indonesia's **constitution**, the country's president and vice president are elected by the people. The president then appoints many other high-level government officials. Members of the legislature, which has two houses, are also elected by the people.

7 Number of presidents in Indonesia's history.

70% Portion of Indonesians who voted in the country's 2014 presidential election.

692 Number of members of Indonesia's legislature.

Indonesia celebrates its national day on August 17. The country first proclaimed its independence on this day in 1945.

CULTURAL GROUPS

I ndonesia has more than 300 different cultural groups. They include groups that have lived in parts of the country for thousands of years and people who have come to Indonesia from other regions more recently. The country's national saying, *Bhinneka tunggal ika*, means "Unity in diversity."

The largest cultural group in Indonesia is the Javanese people. They make up 40 percent of the country's population. Other longtime Indonesian groups include the Sundanese, Malay, Batak, Madurese, and Betawi peoples. The biggest non-Indonesian cultural group is the Chinese. They make up 1.2 percent of the population. Melanesians, who came to Indonesia from some Pacific Ocean island groups, most commonly live on the country's eastern islands.

Wearing traditional masks and dancing in the streets are part of a Javanese harvest celebration.

Indonesians of Chinese descent celebrate the Chinese New Year with lion and dragon dances in January or February.

More than 700 languages are spoken in Indonesia. Bahasa Indonesia is the official language of the country. It is similar to Malay, the official language of the nearby country of Malaysia.

Many other local Indonesian languages are spoken throughout the islands. The most common of these is Javanese. Some Indonesians speak English or Dutch. English is often taught in high schools.

Freedom of religion is part of Indonesia's constitution. Islam is the largest religion in Indonesia. In fact, Indonesia has the largest Muslim population of any country. About 87 percent of Indonesia's people are Muslim. Other religions practiced in Indonesia include Christianity, Hinduism, and Buddhism.

Young Muslims in Indonesia often take religion classes at a mosque, or Muslim house of worship.

Cultural Groups BY THE NUMBERS

13 Number of languages with more than 1 million speakers in Indonesia.

4 Number of hours per week many high school students spend in English classes.

2% Portion of Indonesians who follow the Hindu religion.

ARTS AND ENTERTAINMENT

Indonesia's wide variety of cultures and languages gives the country a diverse arts scene. Storytelling has long been a part of Indonesian cultures, and traditional storytelling is still popular in many parts of the country. Poems and **epic** stories often have never been written down. They are spoken and acted out.

Storytelling traditions in Indonesia have inspired special forms of theater. Puppet shows are common in some parts of the country. Wayang golek uses wooden puppets. In wayang kulit shows, puppeteers use leather devices to cast shadow puppets. Traditional wayang kulit performances sometimes last all night, ending at daybreak.

Indonesian poet and novelist Laksmi Pamuntjak has written national bestsellers set in Indonesia.

Wayang golek is a form of folk art with a long tradition in Indonesia.

Modern Indonesian literature was born in the 1930s. A group of writers joined to publish works in their language, Bahasa Indonesia, and promote the idea of an independent nation. In the 1940s, Chairil Anwar was one of Indonesia's most popular poets. During the period of Guided Democracy, many authors did not have freedom to write what they wished. Some were jailed or forced to leave the country. Today, Indonesian writers are free to tell stories of all kinds.

The most popular type of Indonesian music is called dangdut. It blends traditional styles with popular music from the United States and other parts of the world. Dangdut is played at dance clubs and parties around the country. One Indonesian style featured in many dangdut songs is gamelan music. Gamelans are groups of musicians playing gongs, drums, and other **percussion instruments**. These groups often also feature a stringed instrument, a flute, or a singer.

Jakarta is the center of Indonesian culture today. The city is home to many museums, art galleries, and theaters. The National Museum of Indonesia in Jakarta holds a large collection of **artifacts**, such as tools and statues, from throughout the country's history.

16 Number of films in which dangdut performer Rhoma Irama has starred.

1965– 1979 Years that writer Pramoedya Ananta Toer was jailed by the Indonesian government.

140,000 Number of artifacts in the National Museum of Indonesia.

The bonang is a Javanese musical instrument made of pot-shaped gongs.

SPORTS

Soccer is Indonesia's most popular sport for playing and watching. More than 7 million players are registered with the Football Association of Indonesia. That means they play soccer regularly. Only six other countries have more registered players. Millions of other Indonesians play soccer on fields, in the streets, and in other open spaces throughout the country. The Indonesian national team, formed in 1930, is known as the Red and White. The team has competed in many major tournaments.

Agustin Elya Gradita Retong of Indonesia plays for the national women's basketball team.

Another popular sport in Indonesia is badminton. When the sport was added to the Summer Olympics in 1992, Indonesia took home five medals in badminton. Susi Susanti and Alan Budikusuma, now husband and wife, earned the country's first Olympic gold medals that year. They won the women's and men's singles events. Taufik Hidayat is one of the best players in history. He collected gold medals at the 2004 Olympics and World Championships.

Basketball is a growing sport. Young people and adults around the country play for fun. There are about 100 clubs registered with the Indonesian Basketball Association.

Taufik Hidayat retired from professional competition in 2014.

Martial arts and wrestling are traditional sports in Indonesia. Sisemba is a kick-fighting tradition in which two people fight without using their hands. In pencak silat, a fighter uses every part of the body to beat the opponent.

The people of Madura celebrate their annual harvest with a sport called karapan sapi. *Karapan sapi* means "the race of the bulls." Each person taking part rides a plow pulled by two bulls racing around a field. The sport has been a popular pastime in Madura for thousands of years. Tourists from around the world travel to Madura to watch the races.

Some pencak silat events take place on the beach.

1951

Year the Indonesian Badminton Federation was formed.

190 MILES PER HOUR

Speed of the fastest known overhead shot in badminton, hit by Taufik Hidayat. (305 km per hour)

2

Number of medals won by Indonesia at the 2012 Olympics, both in weightlifting.

18

Number of professional soccer teams in the Indonesia Super League in 2015.

Mapping Indonesia

We use many tools to interpret maps and to understand the locations of features such as cities, states, lakes, and rivers. The map below has many tools to help interpret information on the map of Indonesia.

Map of Indonesia

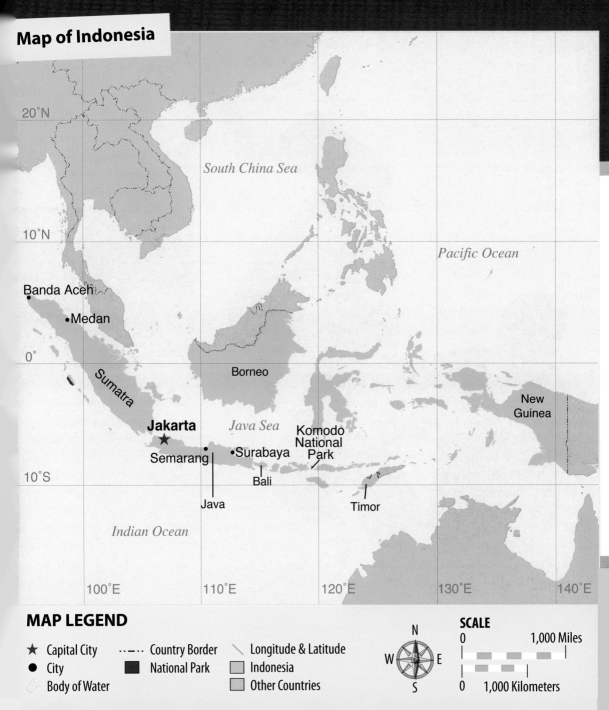

20°N

South China Sea

10°N

Pacific Ocean

Banda Aceh

•Medan

0°

Sumatra

Borneo

New Guinea

Jakarta
★
Semarang

Java Sea

•Surabaya

Komodo National Park

Bali

Java

Timor

10°S

Indian Ocean

100°E   110°E   120°E   130°E   140°E

MAP LEGEND

★ Capital City   ⋅⋅–⋅⋅ Country Border   ╲ Longitude & Latitude
● City   ■ National Park   ▢ Indonesia
◌ Body of Water   ▢ Other Countries

N
W   E
S

SCALE
0 ———————— 1,000 Miles

0   1,000 Kilometers

Mapping Tools

- The compass rose shows north, south, east, and west. The points in between represent northeast, northwest, southeast, and southwest.
- The map scale shows that the distances on a map represent much longer distances in real life. If you measure the distance between objects on a map, you can use the map scale to calculate the actual distance in miles or kilometers between those two points.

- The lines of latitude and longitude are long lines that appear on maps. The lines of latitude run east to west and measure how far north or south of the equator a place is located. The lines of longitude run north to south and measure how far east or west of the Prime Meridian a place is located. A location on a map can be found by using the two numbers where latitude and longitude meet. This number is called a coordinate and is written using degrees and direction. For example, the city of Jakarta would be found at 6°S and 107°E on a map.

Map It!

Using the map and the appropriate tools, complete the activities below.

Locating with latitude and longitude
1. Which island is located at 9°S and 115°E?
2. Which national park is located at 9°S and 119°E?
3. Which city is found at 4°N and 99°E?

Distances between points
4. Using the map scale and a ruler, calculate the approximate distance between Jakarta and Medan.
5. Using the map scale and a ruler, calculate the approximate distance between Banda Aceh and Surabaya.
6. Using the map scale and a ruler, calculate the approximate distance between Jakarta and Semarang.

Quiz Time

Test your knowledge of Indonesia by answering these questions.

1 How many countries have land borders with Indonesia?

2 What is the longest river in Indonesia?

3 How many Javan rhinos are left in nature?

4 What percentage of the world's oil is produced in Indonesia?

5 How many Buddha statues are found at Borobudur?

6 What name was given to the *Homo erectus* fossils discovered in Indonesia in 1891?

7 Who ruled Indonesia after Sukarno and stayed in power until 1998?

8 What is the official language of Indonesia?

9 What is the name for groups of musicians playing gongs, drums, and other kinds of percussion instruments?

10 What does *Karapan sapi* mean?

Key Words

artifacts: objects made or changed by humans

Buddhism: a religion that grew out of the teachings of Gautama Buddha more than 2,500 years ago

constitution: a written document stating a country's basic principles and laws

coup d'état: a sudden overthrow of a government, bringing a new group into power

deforestation: the removal of all the trees from forested land

descendants: people who share common ancestors

dynasty: a series of rulers from the same family

economy: the wealth and resources of a country or area

ecosystems: communities of living things and resources

elevation: the height of land above sea level

empires: groups of territories headed by a single ruler

epic: related to the adventures of a hero or other exciting events

equator: an imaginary circle around Earth's surface that separates the Northern and Southern Hemispheres, or halves, of the planet

exports: sells to other countries

fossils: traces or remains of animals or plants that lived in the distant past

hatchery: a place where eggs are hatched

Hinduism: a religion practiced mainly in India that grew out of the ancient Vedic religion

imports: buys goods from other countries

martial arts: Asian arts of combat and self-defense practiced as a sport

monsoons: steady winds that bring moist air to a region at a certain time of year, causing long periods of heavy rain

percussion instruments: musical instruments sounded by striking, shaking, or scraping

renewable sources: sources of energy that will not run out for billions of years

reserves: resources still unused

species: groups of individuals with common characteristics

subsistence farming: a type of farming that supports the farm family, leaving little or nothing to sell

trading partners: countries that a nation imports goods from and exports goods to

tsunami: a large destructive wave that is often caused by an underwater earthquake

UNESCO: the United Nations Educational, Scientific, and Cultural Organization, whose main goals are to promote world peace and eliminate poverty through education, science, and culture

urban: relating to a city or town

Index

Log on to www.av2books.com

AV² by Weigl brings you media enhanced books that support active learning. Go to www.av2books.com, and enter the special code found on page 2 of this book. You will gain access to enriched and enhanced content that supplements and complements this book. Content includes video, audio, weblinks, quizzes, a slide show, and activities.

AV² Online Navigation

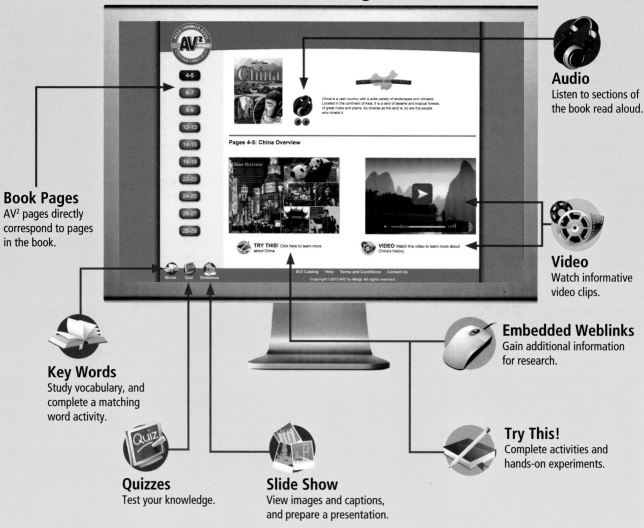

Book Pages
AV² pages directly correspond to pages in the book.

Audio
Listen to sections of the book read aloud.

Video
Watch informative video clips.

Key Words
Study vocabulary, and complete a matching word activity.

Embedded Weblinks
Gain additional information for research.

Quizzes
Test your knowledge.

Slide Show
View images and captions, and prepare a presentation.

Try This!
Complete activities and hands-on experiments.

AV² was built to bridge the gap between print and digital. We encourage you to tell us what you like and what you want to see in the future.

Sign up to be an AV² Ambassador at www.av2books.com/ambassador.